Clean Eating: 30-Day Simple Quick Meal Plan To Boost Your Energy And Stay Healthy

Second Edition

JOHN BROWN

CONTENTS

Introduction

Thank you for purchasing this book, "Amazingly Clean Eating Recipes to Start Your Weight Loss Diet, While Increasing Energy, and Feeling Great!"

Does losing weight always feel like a struggle? Does your workout routine seem to be stressful? Does counting calories feel like a daunting task? If you think it's time to hit the reset button and want to live a much healthier lifestyle without feeling deprived, then Clean Eating Diet is the perfect solution for you.

According to a study published in the journal *Obesity Research & Clinical Practice*, people are 10 percent heavier today than they were in the 1970s—even when they consume the same number of calories and have similar exercise routines. The researchers consider that environmental factors and food that are available in the market nowadays, play key roles on why people today are heavier, even if they consume the same amount of calories and follow the same workout routine.

Poor diet, however, has been identified as the number one contributor to early deaths around the world. A recent analysis from the Institute of Health Metrics and Evaluation (IMHE) states that 21 percent of deaths occur because of an unhealthy diet. According to the research, diets containing high levels of red meat, sugary beverages, and low levels of fruits, vegetables, and whole grains contributed to a higher number of deaths.

While this study may seem alarming, especially if you are into this type of unhealthy diet, the good news is that you can prevent the health risks that come along poor diet by changing your lifestyle. *How can you do this?* One of the best options you have is to follow the *Clean Eating Diet.*

Clean Eating is not like any other diets, but rather, it is a lifestyle that enables you to achieve your health goals through eating nutritious meals. With this diet, there's no need to deprive yourself of flavorful food or to feel a guilty after every meal. All you need to do is to make a major decision to change the way you eat to become healthier.

Clean Eating focuses on changing your eating habits. All you have to do is use the healthiest and freshest ingredients for your meals while limiting your consumption of foods that are lacking in nutrients. And since you don't have to count calories or give up whole food groups, it's very easy to follow. You just need to carefully understand which food will be the best fuel for your own body.

I want to congratulate you for purchasing this book since you're on your first and vital step of becoming healthier. In this book, you will learn about some guidelines about the Clean Eating Diet, and more importantly, this book contains 30 healthy and delectable recipes that are packed with fresh and nutritious ingredients.

It's never been easier to jump-start the journey to a healthier way of life.

What are you waiting for? Let's get started on the path to better eating!

1 Chapter 1: Clean Eating Guidelines

So want to lose weight and be healthier. Now that you're making a full decision to a lasting lifestyle change, it's important to know some guidelines about the Clean Eating Diet. But before that let's clearly define what Clean Eating is.

Like I said earlier, this type of diet isn't complicated like any other popular diets right now. The Clean Eating Diet encourages you to eat whole foods such as vegetables, fruits, whole grains, healthy fat, and good sources of protein. This means that you must limit or restrict yourself from consuming processed, preservative added, packaged, refined, and artificial food. While you can come up with a lengthy list of Clean Eating Diet approved foods, one simple rule of thumb that you must keep in mind is that Clean Eating foods is anything that is fresh, organic, and has barely undergone food processing. Any food item that has ingredients which you can't read or pronounce should be avoided.

To provide you with some other guidelines for this diet, here's a list of some Do's and Don'ts for Clean Eating:

The Do's

- **Drink lots of water everyday**

I know you know how important drinking 8-10 glasses of water every day, but sometimes you just can't help but grab a soda or colored juice drink in replacement for water. But mind you, water has amazing benefits that these sweet drinks can't offer you. Water helps energize your muscles, helps you have a radiant skin, keep your cell healthy, and a lot more; plus it's also good for weight loss too because water as you know, has zero calories.

- **Take frequent small meals**

Yes, you read that right. You can eat at least 5-6 times small meals every day. When you wait for long hours to eat in between breakfast, lunch, and dinner, you get hungrier, thus leading to a better chance of overeating. However, when you eat small meals every four hours, you keep yourself satiated, which helps prevent uncontrollable cravings of unhealthy food.

- **Sweat to shed off the pounds**

No matter how you eat healthy, without proper and regular exercise, you won't achieve that weight that you've always dreamed of. Remember that weight loss is 70% diet and 30% exercise. However, if you're having a hard time going to the gym, just simply be active throughout the day, like cleaning the house, skipping the elevator, or cycling to work.

The Don'ts

- **Never skip breakfast**

Our body needs the energy it needs to burn for the activities we have ahead, that's why breakfast is important so that you will have the fuel to use throughout the day. Plus, eating breakfast would also help you avoid overeating during lunch time.

- **Limit your consumption of sugar**

Most people think that foods that tastes sweet are only the types of food that are considered to be rich in sugar. However, there are some foods and beverages out there that are also loaded with sugar and could cause your blood sugar levels to spike. Some of these are: salad dressing, baked goods made with refined grains and sugars, as well as flavored fruit drinks. Sodas, sports drinks, and even energy drinks, are said to be the largest sources of added sugar in American's diet. Drinking too much of these drinks, may lead to nutrient deficiencies, weight gain, and heart disease.

- **Don't jump into the week without a proper meal plan**

Having a meal plan takes the stress out of not knowing what to eat. When you prepare your own food, you are assured that what you include in the menu are fresh, organic, and nutritious ingredients. With a proper meal plan, you can save more time and money, plus it helps you avoid unhealthy choices of dishes.

Week 1: Remove The Metabolism Death Foods

Metabolism entails everything that your body does to keep you alive, including digesting foods & nutrients, keeping your nerves and brain functioning, eliminating waste, controlling body temperature, circulating blood, and of course, breathing. Since every function in your body relies on energy conversion, an ineffective metabolic function can cause several nasty side effects, such as food sensitivities, digestive issues, weight gain, poor sleeping patterns, mood swings, skin conditions, low energy, headaches, and a lot more. These numerous negative symptoms are the reasons why you need to maintain a proper metabolic function. Everything from sleep deprivation and stress to certain medications and lack of exercise can negatively affect your metabolic function. Because the foods you eat fuel your entire body, it goes without saying that your meal choices can be a major player as well. Let us evaluate some of the most popular metabolism death foods you probably have in your pantry.

Sugar

Given all the possible ways sugar can negatively affect your body, it is no wonder that it is on this list. When you eat sugar, it rapidly enters your bloodstream and creates a spike in glucose levels, triggering your body to store excess fat. This process gradually slows down your metabolism. Studies have shown that diets rich in fructose can result in increased calorie intake, reduced rate of burning these calories, subsequently leading to obesity and weight gain.

Most of the processed foods you take contain hidden sugar, including salad dressings and tomato sauces, and it goes with so many diverse names (maltose, sucrose, dextrose, high fructose corn syrup), that you can be forgiven to mistake it.

"Fat-Free" Foods

Big brands are always marketing "fat free" and "low fat" foods as the healthy way to counter cravings for traditionally high fat foods such as cheeses, desserts, and yogurts, but these foods only tend to replace fats with synthetic sweeteners, which ultimately leads to a sugar rush, followed by increased hunger levels. Since these artificial sweeteners taste like sugar, they make your body think that actual calories are coming, and when they fail to arrive, you start craving sugary foods to compensate for the missing calories.

"Diet" sodas use the same concept. Diet soda drinkers have been associated with increased waist size as compared to non-drinkers. In short, artificial sweeteners, contained in fat free and low fat foods, encourage sugar dependence and sugar craving, ultimately leading to a reduced metabolism. It is much better to go for the full fat variations, and consume them less often.

Commercial Fruit Juice

When it comes to their impact on your metabolism, fruit juices are actually slightly better than sodas. However, they have just about the same negative impact as sugar sweetened drinks, with a single cup of apple juice containing 26 grams of sugar and 110 calories, and a cup of cola containing 26.5 grams of sugar and 105 calories. This means that the juice is actually giving you more calories, with the same level of sugar. While the fruit juice may contain certain minerals and vitamins that are not found in the soda, nutritional content may not be enough to counter the adverse impact on your metabolic function.

What's more, excessive fruit juice consumption has been associated with increased risk of diabetes in adults and childhood obesity.

Salt

Salt is a vital nutrient that your body needs for optimal muscle and nerve function, which is why it is essential to ensure that you get enough in your diet. The dilemma is that most people actually take twice as much as the daily-recommended allowance, 75 percent of which is derived from sub-standard salt added to restaurant and processed foods. Excess sodium leads to retained water in your body, subsequently straining your blood vessels, heart, and kidneys. This can lead to high blood pressure, which can interfere with your entire system, as well as your metabolism.

It is advisable to limit your salt intake from processed foods, and instead take high quality salt like Himalayan pink salt.

Simple Carbohydrates

Your body needs carbohydrates to serve as a source of fuel, give you energy, and facilitate the healthy function of your muscles, brain and heart. However, keep in mind that all carbohydrates are created differently. Generally, try to steer away from white carbs, such as white rice, white pasta, white bread, and baked goods, for instance pastries. These carbohydrates are digested in your body exactly like sugar, and they end up spiking insulin levels and then dropping and slowing down your metabolism. Instead, go for complex carbohydrates that are broken down much slower, leading to sustained energy production for much longer. Incorporate a healthy blend of lentils, sweet potatoes, brown rice, quinoa, whole-wheat pasta, and more, which have also been shown to boost fiber intake. Fiber plays a major role in weight maintenance and weight loss.

Breakfast Cereals

Waking up to a low fat cereal breakfast may feel like you are being healthy, but these tend to lower your metabolism on many levels. These cereals, apart from having questionable additives such as the artificial sweeteners, are just simple carbohydrates. It is ill advised to start your day off with these cereals. Since most people's insulin levels are usually highest in the morning, eating high carb foods will basically lead to a further increase. You will crash long before lunchtime, ultimately giving in to sugary snack cravings. It is much better to start your day with a protein rich meal like eggs, which will keep you satisfied for longer.

Try a Greek Yogurt smoothie or smoked salmon with scrambled eggs for a metabolism enhancing breakfast.

Fast and Processed Foods

It can be demoralizing to start preparing for a healthy dinner after a long day, which is why most people find ready meals and take out foods to be more appealing. However, these meals are prepared with unhealthy fats, white carbs, sugars, and salt, and do not enhance your metabolism. It is advisable to cut back on your excessive fat intake so that you can reap the huge rewards, including reducing the risk of a heart attack, and lessening obesity, in addition to enhanced metabolic function.

Vegetable Oils

In the same way that you need complex carbohydrates and quality salts in your diet, you also require quality fats, such as oily fish, seeds, nuts, and avocadoes. However, unhealthy fats, including certain vegetable oils, can damage your thyroid and endocrine system. Eating these oils usually leads to reduced energy and a slow metabolism. Eliminate the yellow cooking oils such as canola oil, sunflower oil, and soybean oil. Observe food labels carefully and you'll find that these oils are contained in everything, from salad dressings and crackers to pancake mixes and cookies. It is much better to opt for coconut oil for preparing your meals, cook your own baked foods, and use extra virgin olive oil in your dressings to get rid of these awful additives.

Non-Organic Produce

The chemicals contained in pesticides can offset most of your bodily functions, and your metabolism is no exception. Additionally, these chemicals have been associated with reduced metabolic function, as well as increased risk of diabetes and obesity. Go for organic produce whenever possible. Here is a list of twelve of the most pesticide-laden vegetables and fruits:

- Cucumbers

- Sweet Bell Peppers

- Spinach

- Celery

- Grapes

- Strawberries

- Nectarines

- Peaches

- Apples

- Collard Greens

- Kale

- Hot Peppers

- Potatoes

- Snap Peas

- Cherry tomatoes

The Clean fifteen

- Mangos

- Papayas

- Kiwi

- Eggplant

- Asparagus

- Cantaloupe

- Cauliflower

- Grapefruit

- Avocadoes

- Sweet corn

- Pineapples

- Cabbage

- Frozen sweet peas

- Onions

To limit your contact with pesticide, wash and peel all inorganic produce.

Alcohol

Since alcohol is a toxin, your body works tirelessly to remove it from your system as fast as possible. This means that your metabolic functions put a halt to everything else in order to concentrate on getting rid of the alcohol. If you had eaten anything before, the food is automatically stored as fat. Alcohol has been proven to reduce fat burning especially around the stomach, which has notoriously led to the phrase "beer belly". Excessive intake ultimately causes permanent weight gain, and sometimes obesity. However, this does not mean that you have to abstain completely. A glass of wine in the evening is not so bad as we know a little wine is actually good for you. Just limit yourself to one drink or two, and avoid cocktails because these do not work well with your metabolism.

So how can you implement all that in your meals? Here is a sample meal plan to help you get started.

Sample Meal Plan

Below are some meal options you can try

Breakfast

- 2 slices of French toast

- 2 egg vegetable omelet

- Almonds and blueberries plus whole grain cereal

- Toast and half grapefruit

- 2 hardboiled eggs

Snacks

- 1 apple

- 1 cup of yogurt

- 1 fruit bar/whole grain plus 1 cup of yogurt

- Protein powder with 16 ounces of fruit smoothie

Lunch

- 1 vegetable burger

- Tomato wrap and lean deli meat (one to two slices)

- Open face turkey vegetable sandwich

Afternoon snacks

- 15 to 20 almonds

- ¼ cup of sunflower seeds

- ¼ to ½ cup of edamame

- 1 to 2 pieces of string cheese

Dinner

- 1 chicken and spinach enchilada

- 8 to 10 spears of roasted asparagus and 1 portobello mushroom

- Grilled salmon salad with walnuts and pears

Dessert

- 1 berry smoothie popsicle

Week 2: Eat Fat Burning Foods

Your hormone levels, age, gender, genetics, body size & composition, and level of activity influence metabolism. While you may not be able to control all of these factors when you understand them, it is possible and easy to boost your metabolism naturally. Here are some foods that will help you boost your metabolism without even realizing it.

Opt for wholegrain, hearty proteins to boost your metabolism in the morning

Studies have shown that skimping on or skipping breakfast can actually lead to weight gain, since this means that you are more likely to overeat during the day. Here are some of the foods you can include in your breakfast:

Oatmeal (porridge)

This is high in fiber, is satisfying, and can lead to stabilized blood sugar levels because of the slow energy release, which aids in fat loss. It can also help reduce cholesterol levels and eliminate bad fatty acids. Go for unsweetened wholegrain, rolled oats for additional vitamins. Prepare the oatmeal with calcium-rich milk, which serves as a great metabolic trigger. The complex carbohydrates keep your insulin levels low, which minimizes the amount of fat stored by your body. You can improve your oatmeal by adding one or two dashes of cinnamon, which is said to reduce appetite and stabilize blood sugar levels.

Eggs

Studies have shown that eggs take more calories to digest than a cereals (carb-heavy) breakfast. With one egg containing 7g of protein and 75 calories, this may be one the best ways to start your day. The egg yolk contains choline, which can boost fat loss.

A Cup of Fat Burning Green Tea

Green tea has been shown to have a positive effect on metabolism, due to the phytochemical compound known as catechins, with Epigallocatechin gallate (EGCG) being the most abundant. This chemical has been shown to enhance calorie burning, and works in the same way as caffeine, without the increased heartbeat. Caffeinated drinks, such as caffeine, also boost calorie burning by increasing your heart rate. However, keep in mind that adding cream, milk or sweetening the coffee will counteract the effect.

Nutrient Dense and Protein Packed Snacks

Resist the temptation of getting that bag of chips at the vending machine, and go for a healthier choice. Keep in mind that the kind of fat you take matters, and monounsaturated fats are the healthiest alternative. Some of the snacks you should consider in the afternoon or mid-morning include:

* *Water-Based Fruit*

These include apples, pears, grapefruit, grapes, berries, and watermelon. Fruit provides you with minerals and vitamins, in addition to being packed with water and low in calories. Fruit also keeps you full, which will come in handy if you are also looking to lose weight.

* *Greek Yogurt*

Packed with protein and low in sugar, Greek yogurt is an excellent source of energy and nutrition. Protein is the best way to burn more calories and lose weight. It stays longer in your stomach, keeping you satisfied for a prolonged period. In addition, your body has to work extra hard to burn proteins as compared to carbohydrates, which results in more weight loss.

* Raw Vegetables

These are low in calories, and crunch easily. Combine a dish of radishes, raw zucchini, celery, or carrots with your favorite dip for an afternoon or midmorning snack.

* Raw or Roasted Almonds

These are packed with protein, and a handful has been shown to keep off hunger for a long period. However, limit your intake to a handful, as almonds (generally all nuts) are rich in calories.

* Air-Popped Popcorn

While it may seem like consuming 3 cups of popcorn is plenty of food, it is actually very low in calories. Furthermore, since it is packed with fiber, it can fill you up for longer.

Eat a Powerful Lunch

Rather than including protein in your dinner only, ensure that your midday meal is packed with healthy carbs and protein. Suggestions of metabolism boosting foods you can include in your lunch are:

* *Tofu*

While low carb vegetarian protein sources such as tempeh and tofu may not be the conventional protein, they can help boost your metabolism. However, steer away from processed soy products, and stick to the healthier tempeh and tofu soy versions.

* *Turkey or Chicken*

Both of these are rich in protein, which is helpful in boosting metabolism, in addition to helping you build muscles when you exercise. Avoid chicken nuggets, and instead choose the real deal; go for a lean cut, which can be baked or grilled, and throw away the skin. Compliment your grilled chicken breast with some couscous and a side salad for a well-balanced lunch.

* *Salad*

Go for greens that are rich in nutrients, e.g. arugula, or spinach, and combine with a protein such as grilled steak or chicken or a hardboiled egg, and other crunchy vegetables. Spinach salad can not only provide you with protein, but it can also serve you with a whole day's worth of minerals and vitamins. Be cautious when selecting and incorporating salad dressing. Go for low calorie alternatives (such as vinegar and olive oil), and be sure it is packed on the side in order to control the amount that goes to the salad.

* Soup

Instead of cream based soups, go for a clear broth with vegetables and chicken, or perhaps a cold soup such as gazpacho. Soup is said to be a great option for lunch since it is based on water based, which can keep you satisfied with a few calories only. Incorporate more nutrients into your soup by adding V-8 or tomato juice instead of beef or chicken broth. Add turkey or chicken, your favorite veggies, and you will be feeling full for several hours without even consuming plenty of calories.

* Tabouli

This is usually served as a salad, but you can serve it as a side dish or a main course meal. Tabouli is packed with fiber and protein. It has low calorie content, but keeps you satisfied for longer because of the bulgur wheat base.

Take a healthy meal over dinner

It is important to incorporate various metabolism-boosting foods in your dinner. Actually, eating a home prepared, well balanced dinner with your family is less likely to make you overweight or obese. Some of the items you can include in your dinner are:

* Pork

Pork is a great source of protein. Eating more protein takes a longer time to be digested in the stomach. However, stick to lean pork, and avoid the BBQ sauce. Rather, grill it using low fat seasoning, such as herbs.

* Any Lean Meat

Pick a flank steak, top sirloin or eye of round that is packed with

4g of saturated fat at most, per serving. It is advisable to stick to between 3 and 4 ounces of meat.

* Red Meat From Grass Fed Animals as Opposed to Grain Fed Ones

These are rich in Omega 3 fatty acids, which tend to increase your metabolism. It is also high in vitamin E and healthy fat. Ensure you stick to lean meat for its healthy benefits.

* Tuna

Grilled tuna steak is a great idea for a nice low calorie meal or BBQs, or you can also blend it in a sandwich and eat with whole grain bread for a cheaper alternative.

* Fish

Fish is among the best protein sources, and it has even been shown to be more satisfying than beef or chicken. The main reason why fish is very popular is because it is packed with omega 3 fatty acids, which have been shown to counter heart disease and various other chronic conditions. Keep it low fat by BBQing it or grilling it.

* *Quinoa*

This protein-based grain has been a favorite for vegetarians for years, with one cup containing 5g of fiber, and 8g of protein. Quinoa is also packed with vitamin E, selenium, zinc, and iron.

* *Beans*

Beans deliver a triple punch, since they are a protein, a vegetable, and an excellent source of fiber, with one cup containing 15g of protein, 4g of fat, and 12g of fiber.

Sample Meal Plan

Breakfast

- 2 slices of multi grain toast with one tablespoon of peanut butter

- 1 cup of milk

- 1 cup of regular tea or coffee with milk and one teaspoon of sugar

Snack

- Water

- 3 crackers

- ½ cup of toasted almonds

Lunch

- ½ cup of sliced cucumbers

- 1 cup of yogurt

- 1 smoked chicken sandwich with bread: flavored mayo, sliced cucumber, 5 strips of red bell peppers, 2 slices of low fat Swiss cheese

Snack

- ½ cup of baby carrots

- 1 medium banana

Dinner

- Fresh fruit cocktail salad

- Couscous with spring veggies

- 1 cup of milk

Week 3: Interval Exercise To Boost Your Energy

We cannot talk about ways to boost your energy level without talking about exercising. Exercising is great as it works your muscles helping you burn fat, increasing your energy levels and definitely keeping you healthy. Sure, you are aware that an hour's practice of jiu-jitsu, an afternoon bike ride, or a solid weight training session will crank up your metabolism. The only problem is; what are the best strategies to not only enhance your metabolism but to keep it going throughout the day? At its most basic definition, metabolism is a range of chemical processes through which your body cells produce the energy and substances required to sustain life.

Undoubtedly, putting on and maintaining lean muscle mass is the most effective way to boost your metabolism. Muscle comprises of what is referred to as metabolically active tissue, meaning that it is built, utilized and maintained using energy, as compared to fat tissue, which is basically dormant and does not burn any calories. Weight training is the best way to increase muscle mass, meaning that even if your goal is to boost your energy, weight training should always be a part of your plan. Below are amazing workouts to boost your energy.

HIIT

If you have ever tried High-Intensity Interval Training (HIIT), you are probably aware that 15 minutes of these exercises is no walk in the park.

During exercise, it is physiologically impossible to maintain maximal intensities for a prolonged period due to the way your body uses fuel; hence, the exercises do not last for too long making such exercises great for people who just want to exercise for a short time. Below are the stages that your body goes through during HIIT.

Stage One: Phosphocreatine

The first ten to twenty seconds will be great! You'll be sprinting like a zebra! This is because you are utilizing a high-intensity source of energy called phosphocreatine.

Stage Two: Anaerobic Glycolysis and Lactic Acid

Your phosphocreatine levels start running low after approximately twenty seconds, and anaerobic glycolysis takes precedence. Here, your body produces more lactic acid and uses it as a source of fuel. While you will still be running as fast as possible, your lungs will be working extra hard and you'll start slowing down. If you are a gifted speed skater or a member of the Jamaican Olympic Steeplechase team, you might be able to sustain this for about ten minutes. Otherwise, you would need to cut down your speed, and even slow down to a halt.

Oxygen – The Magic Ingredient

One of the reasons why you'd fail at the twenty-minute sprint challenge is the demand and supply of oxygen when using up so much energy. Nature is known for trade-offs, and in this case, you're trading efficiency for intensity. Aerobic metabolism takes precedence when you are working at a lower intensity (for example during a simple stroll). Your body breaks down fat and carbohydrates for energy with the help of oxygen. While this may be extremely efficient, it prevents you from working at top speed. Aerobic metabolism gives you efficiency while sacrificing on intensity. In the past, this would have come in handy for traveling long distances as you forage for water or food.

On the other hand, anaerobic metabolism takes precedence when you are working at a higher intensity (for example sprinting). Your body cannot transport oxygen to where it is needed fast enough. While this is extremely inefficient, it allows you to produce short surges of high-energy or speed, which would've come in handy when escaping a rock-wielding Grok or a sabre-toothed tiger.

So, these are the two systems with which you operate, with their own merits and demerits. However, what if you could have your cake and still eat it?

This is where High-Intensity Interval Training comes in. HIIT enables you to vary intervals of lower intensity (for instance one minute of walking) with short bursts of high-intensity exercise (for instance ten to twenty seconds of sprinting).

- The periods of higher intensity produce a metabolic demand that's very handy for overall conditioning and prolonged fat loss.

- The periods of lower intensity allow you to recover, and utilize the aerobic energy method.

There are several ways to perform HIIT. The main thing you should keep in mind is the primary principle: vary periods of low intensity with short bursts of high intensity.

Weighted Circuits

Resistance exercises are one of the most effective ways to do HIIT. Go for compound exercises that utilize oxygen very well, for instance:

- Dumbbell snatch plus wrestler's sprawl. Here is a link showing you how to do this

- Hang clean plus front squat plus overhead press

- Perform a pull-up, drop down and do a push-up, then do another pull-up, repeat, and so forth.

- Jumping squats

- Snatches or kettlebell swings

- Burpees

- Carrying a dense sandbag for speed

- Sprint up a slanted hill, and then perform a rapid set of pushups while at the top

- Alternate 100 meter sprints with a set of dumbbell swings

For you to sustain your body's energy demands for this week, you will need to eat well. Here is a sample meal plan to help you to achieve just that.

Sample Meal Plan

Breakfast

- ¾ cup of high fiber cereal (granola, bran, etc.)

- 1 cup of milk

- 1 cup of regular tea or coffee and 1 teaspoon of sugar

Snack

- Water

- 3 melba toasts with two slices of cheese

Lunch

- 1 small peach

- ½ cup of zucchini slices

- ½ cup of celery sticks

- 1 tuna sandwich with two slices of bread: ¼ cup of tuna, blended with 1 tablespoon of light mayo, red bell pepper, chopped celery, and salt & pepper to taste

Afternoon snack

- 1 small plum

- 1 cup of yogurt

Dinner

- 1 small orange

- Green beans sautéed in garlic oil – 250mL (1 cup) per person

- Whole grain noodles with beef

- 1 cup of milk

Week 4: Take Supplements To Boost Your Energy

Your morning black coffee or latte may give you a short-term boost of energy but leave you feeling down after some time. Remember that even though caffeine can stimulate you and give you some energy, it also strains the endocrine system and adrenal glands. Energy drinks are also not great since they are packed with sugar and other short-lived stimulants such as caffeine. Just like the effects of sugar in cereal, sugar, and other low-nutrition snacks, excessive consumption of caffeine can lead to dependence and energy crashes. Consistent energy depends on 3 factors: exercise, sleep, and eating natural and organic foods. Here are ten supplements you should try to help your body get rid of toxins:

* *Iodine*

Hormones control metabolism and trigger the production of the several biochemicals linked to energy creation. Iodine is used by the thyroid to form thyroxine (T4) and triiodothyronine (T3), the two hormones responsible for regulating all the other hormones. Dark leafy greens, sea vegetables (wakame, kombu, arame, dulse seaweed), and seafood are the best dietary iodine sources. You can also take iodine supplements such as nascent or colloidal iodine.

* Vitamin B12

All the cells in your body need B12 for metabolism. In fact, it is required by the whole cellular energy creation, referred to as Kreb's cycle or the Citric Acid cycle. The dilemma is that your body requires dietary sources in order to create B12, as it cannot produce it on its own. The best natural sources are dairy, red meat, mussels, and clams. It is safe to supplement with B12, since it does not have any upper dietary limit or side effects. The supplement versions are adenosylcobalamin and methylcobalamin.

* Melatonin

The pineal gland releases the hormone melatonin, and directly affects energy metabolism. People who are short of melatonin suffer from accelerated brain aging and fatigue. Melatonin levels have also been shown to influence the effects of genes on your health and gene activation. The good news is that melatonin is released by the pineal gland when nighttime darkness approaches. Studies have shown that sleeping with the lights on tends to interfere with the production of melatonin. Inconsistent bedtime can lead to a melatonin imbalance, which can in turn interfere with your blood sugar, energy levels, and sometimes weight.

* Ginkgo Biloba

For a long time, Ginkgo has been known to be a powerful antioxidant as well as effective at enhancing blood flow. A recent review also suggests that it can improve cellular energy (ATP) production and mitochondrial respiration in your brain cells. This stabilizes metabolic activity in your cells, protecting them and enhancing longevity and general health. When it comes to supplements, go for those with the least fillers.

* CoQ10 in cell fuzion TM

This is a major player in the creation of cellular energy. CoQ10 is found in every cell in your body, although such organs as the liver, kidneys and the heart contain higher concentrations. However, a deficiency is not impossible. One of the most common symptoms of its deficiency is fatigue, although blood sugar imbalance, stomach ulcers, and high blood pressure can also appear. Such supplements as Cell Fuzion can provide the necessary materials for boosting CoQ10.

* Female Fuzion ^{TM} and Androtrex

Hormone imbalances are followed by exhaustion and fatigue. In the modern world of poor dietary options and environmental toxins, balancing hormones has become more of a juggling act. Such herbs as muira puama, tongkat ali, ashwagandha, and tribulus terrestris facilitate endocrine organs like the adrenal glands, pancreas, thyroid, testes, and ovaries. You can find these herbs as individual supplements, but their complementary effects makes such herbal blends as Female Fuzion ^{TM} and Androtrex ideal supplement options.

* Acetyl L-carnitine

L-carnitine is another biochemical needed for energy metabolism. It is responsible for transporting fatty acids to the mitochondria to be converted into energy. Mitochondrial energy creation is also boosted by acetyl groups.

Now that you know what you should be eating and what not to eat let's now look at a few recipes that you can try today.

2 Chapter 2: Energy-Boosting Breakfast Recipes

Let's face it. It's really hard for almost everyone to wake up early in the morning to prepare food for breakfast, resulting for a drive-thru in fast food restaurants or simply missing the most important meal of the day. However, skipping breakfast can be very harmful to your clean eating lifestyle. *Why would that be possible when I haven't even added a calorie on my body?*

But tell you what, this often leads to excessive eating of snacks or disproportionate meals during lunch and dinner. I know, there's one more thing that drives you nuts, and that is thinking, *eating healthy means being stuck on tasteless menus.* Well, worry no more, the breakfast recipes in this chapter are surely delectable, satisfying, will give you a surge of energy, and more importantly, are healthy; most of them are easy to make too!

Tortilla with eggs and beans

Ingredients

- 1 scallion, sliced

- 3 teaspoons canola oil divided

- ¼ teaspoon salt divided

- 1 (15-ounce) can of pinto beans, rinsed

- 8 (6-inch) corn tortillas

- ¾ cup of shredded sharp Cheddar cheese

- 1 ½ cups of romaine lettuce, very thinly sliced

- 2 tablespoons of chopped fresh cilantro

- ½ cup of prepared green salsa

- Canola oil cooking spray

- 2 teaspoons of lime juice

- 4 large eggs

- ¼ teaspoon of pepper, freshly ground & divided

Procedure

Preheat oven to 400 degrees F. Mix 1/8 teaspoon of pepper, 1/8 teaspoon of salt, lime juice, 1 teaspoon of oil, cilantro, scallion, and lettuce in a bowl, and set aside. Combine salsa and beans in a separate bowl.

Brush the cooking spray on either side of the tortillas, and place them on a large baking sheet in four sets of overlying pairs. Scoop approximately one-third cup of the bean mix and spread over the tortillas. Sprinkle each with three tablespoons of cheese.

In the meantime, add the two teaspoons of oil left in a large nonstick skillet over medium heat. Beat the eggs in a small bowl, and then add them to the pan. Season with the remaining salt and pepper.

Lower the heat and cook for five to seven minutes while undisturbed until set.

Assemble by placing an egg over each tortilla pair, and top with a quarter cup of the lettuce mix.

Servings: 4

Breakfast taco

Ingredients

- 1 tablespoon of salsa

- ½ cup of liquid egg substitute

- 2 corn tortillas

- 2 tablespoons of shredded reduced-fat Cheddar cheese

Procedure

Top the tortillas with cheese and salsa. Slide into the microwave and heat for about thirty seconds or until the cheese has melted.

In the meantime, spread cooking spray around a small nonstick skillet, and heat over medium-high heat. Stir in your egg substitute, and cook while stirring until cooked through, approximately ninety seconds. Split the scrambled eggs among the tacos.

Serves: 2

Egg in Marinara Dressing

Gear up for this exciting meal packed with protein and essential nutrients.

Ingredients

2 fresh eggs

1/2 finely sliced onion

crushed red pepper

1 cup marinara sauce

2 whole wheat pita pocket

Procedure

1. Lightly toast the pita pocket in an oven toaster. Set aside.

2. Pour in olive oil in a small frying pan over medium heat.

3. Sauté onion until golden or brown.

4. Season with pepper and add the marinara sauce. Crack the eggs onto the mixture, then let it simmer.

5. Serve with pita pockets.

Serves: 2

Calories: 306 per serving

Baked Mushroom with Baby Spinach

Eating mushrooms can help you prevent breast cancer, high cholesterol levels, and prostate cancer. Spinach on the other hand, is loaded with protein, fiber, and vitamins A, C, E, and B6. Try this mushroom-spinach combo recipe for a nutritious breakfast!

Ingredients

2 slices of whole-wheat bread, toasted

1 cup mushrooms, cut into slices

4 tbsp. onion, chopped

3 tbsp. red bell pepper, sliced

2 cups baby spinach

4 organic eggs

salt and black pepper to taste

Procedure

1. Preheat oven to 450°F.

2. Coat a large pan with cooking spray. Sauté the mushrooms, onion, and bell pepper, and baby spinach for about 5 minutes.

3. Stir 4 eggs with ½ cup skim milk.

4. Pour over toasted bread then top with sautéed vegetables. Add desired amount of Parmesan cheese.

5. Bake for about 15 minutes.

6. Serve.

Serves: 2

Calories: 290 per serving

Cinnamon and Oats Bowl

Break every bleak weather and warm your tummy with this tasty treat.

Ingredients

2 tsp. cinnamon, freshly ground

8 tsp. brown sugar

3 cups rolled oats, organic

½ cup raisins

½ cup walnuts, chopped

low-fat milk (optional)

Procedure

1. Prepare your organic oats according to package directions.

2. In a mixing bowl, combine brown sugar and cinnamon. Pour over the oats.

3. Add walnuts and raisins. Stir well.

4. Splash milk if desired.

Serves: 10

Calories: 327 per 1 cup serving

Coco-Quinoa Burgoo with Strawberry

Bored with the usual oats for breakfast? Try this porridge topped with shredded coconut and strawberries.

Ingredients

6 tbsp. coconut oil

1 tsp. cinnamon, finely ground

½ cup quinoa, well rinsed

½ cup light coconut milk (preferably organic)

½ cup low-fat milk

2 tsp. maple syrup

3 tsp. shredded coconut, unsweetened

½ cup strawberries, freshly sliced

Procedure

1. Over medium heat, drizzle oil in a saucepan.

2. Add cinnamon, then quinoa and stir persistently until smoothly covered.

3. Spill both coconut and low-fat milk in the pan. Bring to a simmer until milk has been fully blended in the mixture.

4. Drizzle with maple syrup and then transfer into a bowl. Top with shredded coco and strawberries.

Serves: 2

Calories: 150 per serving

Chia Soleil Pudding

Did you know that chia seeds contain more Omega 3-s than a regular salmon? Surprised? Well, this magical seed has more to offer!

Ingredients

1 ½ cups almond milk

4 tbsp. chia seeds

1 tsp. maple syrup

½ cup fresh blueberries

For toppings:

1 ripe mango, freshly sliced

6 fresh blueberries

Procedure

1. Whip all the ingredients together in a large bowl except the toppings.

2. Cover and chill in the fridge for about 3 hours.

3. Remove and add up the toppings.

4. Serve and enjoy every spoonful of it!

Serves: 2

Calories: 110 per serving

Kiwi and Banana Super Bowl

Power-up each morning with this super bowl, loaded with dietary fiber that aids digestion and enhances weight loss.

Ingredients

½ cup almond milk, unsweetened

4 tbsp. ripe mango, frozen

4 tbsp. avocado, cut into cubes for easy blending

½ cup kale

½ cup spinach

3 ice cubes

¼ cup water (add more if preferred)

For the toppings:

1 regular banana, chopped

1 medium size sliced kiwi

1 tbsp. coco flakes

Procedure

1. In a clean blender, mix all the smoothie ingredients until evenly blended.

2. Pour in a medium sized bowl and top with banana, kiwi, and coconut flakes.

3. Serve and dig in this irresistible smoothie.

Serves: 1

Calories: 170 per serving

Creamy Salmon-Capers

Need a speedy savory satisfaction for your hectic morning schedule?
You've got the perfect meal on this one.

Ingredients

½ cup cream cheese

100 g flaked salmon (cooked or canned)

1 tbsp. capers, well drained

1 tsp. lemon zest

1 whole-grain pita

1 tomato, thinly sliced into four

1 cup fresh arugula leaves

¼ cup water (add more if preferred)

Procedure

1. Combine cheese and capers in a small bowl.

2. Add the lemon zest. Stir well.

3. Spread the mixture half of the pita, then top with salmon
   flakes, tomato and arugula.

4. Fold and slice into two.

5. Best served with Chia Soleil Pudding.

Serves: 2

Calories: 105 per serving

Nutty Cookies with a Twist

Bored with the usual cookies with nuts? Try this recipe with added banana for a good source of omega-3 fatty acids, Vitamin E, and B Vitamins.

Ingredients

½ cup oats

1 egg, beaten

6 tbsp. low-fat milk

1 medium-sized banana, mashed

1tbsp. raisins

1 tbsp. flaxseed, finely ground

1tbsp. walnuts, chopped

1 tsp. honey

1tsp cinnamon

salt to taste

Procedure

1. Preheat the oven to 350 °F.

2. Place the oats in a blender until powdered.

3. In a large bowl, whisk all the ingredients together.

4. Coat a baking sheet with non-stick spray.

5. Scoop a batter on the sheet.

6. Bake for about 15 minutes. Serve.

Serves: 2

Calories: 150 per serving

Slow-cooked Sorghum in Pumpkin Purée

Prepare in the evening and get ready to wake-up for a bowl of whole-grain with high levels of antioxidant.

Ingredients

2 cups sorghum, thoroughly rinsed

2 cups almond milk

2 cups water

1 ½ cups pumpkin purée

2 tbsp. pumpkin pie, spiced

2 tsp. vanilla extract

Procedure

1. Combine all ingredients in a slow cooker.

2. Stir well and let it simmer over low fire for 8 hours.

3. Serve.

Serves: 8

Calories: 221 per serving

Rainbow Acai in a Jar

Enjoy a breakfast filled with colorful fruits on jars that even kids will surely love!

Ingredients

2 packs acai purée, frozen

1 regular banana

1 mango, finely sliced

1 kiwi, cubed

2 tbsp. nuts, unsalted and chopped

1 cup fresh raspberries

1tbsp. coconut, unsweetened and shredded

4tbsp coconut milk

¼ cup water

Procedure

1. In a food processor or blender, combine acai, milk, and water. Blend well until you achieve a smooth consistency.

2. Pour in the mixture evenly on jars then layer fruits, nuts and coconut.

3. Cover and freeze to fridge.

Serves: 2

Calories: 296 per serving

3 Chapter 3: Spice-up Every Lunch with Healthy Fully-loaded Meals

Not sure what to eat during lunch time? You don't have to stick with the usual salad in the office. Satisfy and fill your stomach with these delectable meals that's below 500 calories.

Chile-crusted scallops with cucumber salad

Ingredients

Salad

- ½ cup of cashews salted roasted & coarsely chopped

- 2 teaspoons of lemon juice

- ¼ cup of coarsely chopped flat-leaf parsley

- 2 medium cucumbers

- 2 thinly sliced scallions, (white & light green parts)

- ¼ cup of extra-virgin olive oil

- 1/8 teaspoon of salt

Scallops

- 2 tablespoons of minced seeded serrano chile

- ½ teaspoon of kosher salt

- 1 teaspoon of cumin seeds

- 1 teaspoon of freshly cracked black pepper

- ¼ pounds of dry sea scallops

Procedure

For the salad: peel the cucumbers, and seed them. Divide them lengthwise and slice into quarter inch thick pieces. Combine the parsley, oil, lemon juice, scallions, cashews, cucumbers and salt in a large bowl.

For the scallops: Toss the cumin seeds into a small skillet and toast them over medium high heat or until fragrant, approximately one minute. Place on a cutting board and allow to cool before chopping coarsely. Combine the salt, pepper, chile, and cumin seeds in a small bowl. Drain the scallops, then pat and rub using the spice mixture. Thread scallops on 4-quarter inch skewers.

Warm your grill to medium high, and spray the grill rack with oil. Grill scallops for approximately four minutes per side. Remove scallops carefully and serve warm with cucumber salad.

Servings: 4

Hearty Ham Sandwich

The whole family will flip for this yummy and hearty meal, loaded with cheesy ham.

Ingredients

1tsp. butter

4 mushrooms, thinly sliced

4 slices whole-wheat bread

4 slices Swiss cheese

4 slices roasted ham, uncured

Procedure

1. Preheat a panini press.

2. Melt butter in a skillet over medium heat.

3. Sauté mushrooms until golden. Set aside.

4. Layer the remaining ingredients between bread slices.

5. Place the ham sandwich in a panini press until well toasted.

6. Serve.

Serves: 4

Calories: 280 per serving

Green Leafy Wraps

Be amazed with this meat-tasting wraps that's actually made with pure veggies. Don't believe me? Taste it for yourself!

Ingredients

1tsp. butter

4 cups walnuts, coarsely ground

2 tbsp. cumin, finely ground

3 tsp. chili powder

3 tsp. coriander powder

4 tbsp. tamari

12 large collard leaves

salsa (homemade or from grocery stores)

Procedure

1. Combine all ingredients (except leaves) in a large bowl.

2. Spoon a mixture in the middle portion of the leaf, then top with salsa.

3. Roll the leaf ala burrito.

4. Repeat step with the remaining filling and leaves. Serve.

Serves: 12

Calories: 275 per serving

Potato Pizza

Who says you can't have pizza when on a diet? Munch this mouthwatering cheesy crust up until the last bite!

Ingredients

6 medium-sized sweet potatoes, mashed

2 cups almond flour

1 cup pizza sauce

1 cup cheese (preferably mozzarella)

2 tsp. baking soda

2 tbsp. Italian seasoning

1 tsp. salt

toppings of your choice (ham, tomatoes, bacon)

Procedure

1. Set oven to 450 °F.

2. In a serving bowl, mix in potatoes, baking soda, flour, seasoning, and salt.

3. Mold using your hands, until mixture forms a pizza dough.

4. Line a parchment paper in a pizza pan.

5. Bake for about 20 minutes.

6. Slice up and enjoy!

Serves: 4

Calories: 351 per serving

A Taste of the Caribbean

Eat up with a dish that's bursting with flavors of lime and different spices.

Ingredients

1 tuna steak, cooked and sliced into pieces

½ cup vegetable broth

½ cup mango, diced

½ red bell pepper, chopped

4 tbsp. scallions, finely cut

2 tbsp. cilantro

3 tsp. peanut butter

1 ½ tsp. rice wine vinegar

1 ½ tsp. lime juice, freshly squeezed

2 butterhead lettuce

½ cup vegetable broth

Procedure

1. Toss tuna, scallions, cilantro, and mango in a bowl. Set aside.

2. In another container, combine wet ingredients. Add to tuna mixture.

3. Add salt and pepper to add flavor.

4. Arrange lettuce leaves on a large plate, then put the mixture in each.

Serves: 2

Calories: 260 per serving

Shrimp in Collards

You can't resist eating this shrimp recipe for lunch after a busy morning.

Ingredients

1 kl. shrimp, peeled and deveined (remove tail if preferred)

½ kl. fresh collard greens, finely chopped

4 medium-sized shallots or any onions, thinly sliced

4 turkey sausages

4 tbsp. scallions, finely cut

2 tbsp. olive oil (divide into two)

1 tsp. spice mixture or herbs

½ tsp. sea salt

1 tsp. paprika

1 tsp. chili powder

ground black and cayenne pepper to taste

Procedure

1. Toss last five ingredients in a small bowl.

2. In a separate container, mix shrimp with herbs.

3. Prepare a medium wok, and put over medium-high fire.

4. Heat 1 tbsp. olive oil. Stir onions, shrimp, until turns pink in color. Set aside.

5. Cook sausage in the remaining oil until golden. Layer collard greens in the pan then cover for about 2 minutes.

6. Add the shrimp mixture and cook for 1 more minute.

7. Serve while hot.

Serves: 8

Calories: 268 per serving

Fruity Detox Drink

Sweet and creamy detox drink? Why not? Feel good inside and out!

Ingredients

1 cup raspberries

2 bananas, diced

1 kiwi, cut into slices

2 fresh oranges

1 cup ripe mango, frozen and chopped

¾ cup Acai purée

1 cup coco milk, unsweetened

2 fresh mint leaves

2 scoops vanilla pea, powdered

Procedure

1. Place all listed ingredients in a clean blender or a food processor.

2. Blend until you achieve a smooth consistency.

3. Pour into a mason jar or glass. Serve immediately.

Serves: 2

Calories: 342 per serving

Savory Steak with Salsa

Heat your taste buds with this must-try dish —a signature classic steak recipe paired with salsa.

Ingredients

olive oil cooking spray

2 tbsp. olive oil

½ kilo tenderloin steak, well washed

6 tomatoes, cut into half

6 tbsp. freshly squeezed lemon juice

2 minced garlic

1 cup cilantro leaves, chopped

black pepper, freshly ground

salt to taste

1 summer squash, cut lengthwise making 4 slices

1 fresh zucchini, slice into four

2 onions, slice into two

2 jalapeño pepper, seed removed and cut in half

Procedure

1. Preheat oven to 475 °F.

2. Prepare 2 large roasting pans and coat with cooking spray.

3. Arrange tomatoes and last four ingredients on the pans.

4. Place in the oven and roast for about 12 minutes.

5. For the dressing, put in lime juice, and garlic, salt and pepper, and cilantro in a small mixing bowl. Set aside.

6. Remove veggies from oven and let it cool for a while.

7. Cut vegetables into cubes and carefully combine them with the dressing in another container.

8. Pour dressing over chopped salsa and chill in the fridge.

9. Over medium fire, heat olive oil in a non-stick pan. Season the steak (both sides) with salt and pepper and cook in the pan for about 4 minutes on each side.

10. Serve on a large plate with a cup of veggie salsa on the side.

Serves: 8

Calories: 204 per serving

Asian-style Broccoli Noodles

Yin and yang, a famous concept of Asian cuisine which represents a perfect balance. This Asian inspired recipe has that for you— the perfect balance of flavors in a noodle dish.

Ingredients

1 tsp. olive oil

2 cups whole-wheat spaghetti noodles

10 crowns, broccoli florets

2 oranges, freshly squeezed and zested

2 cups snow peas, trimmed

4 tbsp. soy sauce

½ tsp. red pepper flakes

8 cloves minced garlic

2 tbsp. ginger, grounded

Procedure

1. In a large pot, boil water and put noodles. Stir occasionally.

2. Add broccoli and simmer for about five minutes.

3. Remove from water and transfer to a bowl. Set aside.

4. Place orange zest and juice, soy sauce, ginger and pepper flakes in a small bowl. Whisk thoroughly.

5. Heat a large non-stick skillet over medium heat. Cook beef, then add peas and the mixture from the small bowl.

6. Pour in beef mixture to spaghetti and toss carefully, until well coated.

Serves: 8

Calories: 379 per serving

Tasty Turkey Tacos

This is the perfect whole-grain meal to keep your tummy full and happy.

Ingredients

6 corn tortillas

½ kilo ground lean turkey

1 cup black beans

1 bundle romaine lettuce

½ cup salsa

olive oil cooking spray

ground black pepper and salt to taste

Procedure

1. Preheat oven to 350°F.

2. Wrap tortillas in foil, to make 2 packets.

3. Place on a baking sheet and bake for about 15 minutes.

4. Over medium fire, coat a non-stick pan with cooking spray.

5. Season turkey with salt and pepper, then cook until browned.

6. Remove foil from packets and lay to plates.

7. Distribute lettuce, turkey, beans, and salsa evenly on corn tortillas.

8. Fold or create a wrap and serve warm.

Serves: 3

Calories: 276 per serving

Crabby-Avocado Salad

A protein-packed dish paired with avocado, providing a great creamy texture on every bite.

Ingredients

4 regular-sized avocado, sliced

½ kilo lump crabmeat, cooked

8 hard boiled eggs, cut into slices

4 tomatoes, chopped

4 shredded butter leaf lettuce

1 cup black beans

1 thinly sliced fennel bulb

2 carrots, finely chopped

For the dressing:

1 cup buttermilk

2 cups Greek yogurt (nonfat)

½ cup chili sauce

4 tbsp. onion, grated

1 clove minced garlic

1 tsp. cayenne pepper, grounded

4 tbsp. fresh parsley, finely chopped

½ tsp. salt

Procedure

1. In a medium-sized bowl, mix all the ingredients for the dressing and set aside.

2. On a large plate, lay lettuce (or your choice of individual serving) and top with tomatoes, eggs, carrot, fennel, crab, and avocado.

3. Serve with dressing.

Serves: 8

Calories: 246 per serving

4 Chapter 4: Clean Eating Dinner Recipes under 300 Cal

Mac n' Cheese Overload

Macaroni and cheese? We all know the winning pair!

Ingredients

1 ½ cup elbow macaroni (whole-grain)

1 ½ oz. roasted ham, finely diced

1 oz. mushrooms (preferable cremini), finely sliced

1 ½ tsp. brown-rice flour

1 cups low-fat milk (divide into two half cups)

1 cup Swiss cheese, grated

1/2 tbsp. mustard

1 tsp. olive oil

1 tsp. butter, unsalted

1 small onion, sliced

sea salt and black pepper to taste

herbs of your choice for garnishing

Procedure

1. Cook macaroni according to packaging instructions.

2. Heat oil in a large pan on medium-high.

3. Sauté onion and ham until browned, then add the mushroom.

4. Sprinkle with flour, and season with salt, and pepper.

5. Add mustard and ½ cup milk. Stir well.

6. Gradually add the remaining ½ cup milk, and stir constantly until sauce is thickened.

7. Remove from heat and mix in cheese macaroni.

8. Serve with your fave herb.

Serves: 3

Calories: 299 per serving

Lamb Côtelette with Pear Sauce

Taste a dish that may have come from a high-end restaurant with this lamb loin recipe.

Ingredients

8 medium-sized lamb loin chops (trim fat)

1 ripe pear, peeled and cut into slices

½ cup apple juice

3 tsp. balsamic vinegar

½ cup beef broth

1 ½ tsp. rosemary and thyme, finely chopped

½ tsp. salt

½ tsp. ground black pepper

Procedure

1. Generously season the lamb with salt and pepper.

2. Heat a large skillet over medium-high heat, and cook lamb until golden. Set aside.

3. Remove any fat from skillet, and return to cooking over medium heat. Add pear, apple juice, balsamic, and broth and let it simmer for about 3 minutes.

4. Remove from heat and mix in the herbs rosemary and thyme.

5. Top the well-cooked lamb with pear sauce, and serve.

Serves: 4

Calories: 230 per serving

Orange Roast Salmon with Rosemary and Thyme

The classic ingredient combination of rosemary and thyme allow the palatable flavor of the salmon to shine through.

Ingredients

cooking spray

4 shallots, discard outer layer

9 radishes, cut into two

1 ½ cups salmon fillets, deboned

1 ½ tsp. olive oil

2 tsp. basil, chopped (fresh mint as alternative)

1 tsp. rosemary and thyme, finely chopped

1 fresh orange, thinly sliced

½ tsp. salt

½ tsp. ground black pepper

Procedure

1. Set the oven to 425°F.

2. Cover a large baking sheet with foil and coat with cooking spray.

3. Lightly place shallots and radishes. Then drizzle with oil.

4. Sprinkle with salt and pepper to taste.

5. Carefully toss and spread within the one layer.

6. Add the chopped rosemary and thyme and roast for about 15 minutes.

7. Press the veggies to edges of baking sheet and place the salmon in the middle part. Use the sliced orange to cover each fillet.

8. Return in the oven and continue roasting for about 20 minutes.

9. Remove the salmon from the oven, discarding the orange slices.

10. Toss with the freshly squeezed orange juice. Serve.

Serves: 2

Calories: 244 per serving

Seven Veggies with White Fish

Give this fish and veggie recipe a try; it will surely be a hit!

Ingredients

2 large potatoes, diced

2 regular-sized turnips, sliced

2 large carrots, cut into cubes

1 large zucchini, diced

1 red bell pepper, well chunked

1 cup green beans, cut into two

½ fresh green cabbage, sliced into about an inch size

1 kl. tilapia (or any whitefish), chunked

1 cup fresh cilantro, finely chopped

1 ½ cups chickpeas, canned and well drained

½ cup raisins

3 cloves minced garlic

1 tsp. chili paste

2 tbsp. spice mix

2 tbsp. olive oil

1 tsp. salt

Procedure

1. Heat olive oil in a large stew over medium fire.

2. Sauté garlic with spice mix until golden brown.

3. Add the first five ingredients in the pot and pour in water to fully cover veggies. Simmer for about 30 minutes.

4. Add in salt, beans, pepper, and chili paste and cook for another 15 minutes.

5. When cooked, cool it for about 10 minutes.

6. Pour the vegetable mixture in a blender or food processor until a soft-paste consistency is achieved.

7. Bring the mixture back on stew.

8. Add raisins, chickpeas, and fish. Cook and cover until fish meat flakes smoothly on fork. The fish will now steam on top of the veggie mixture.

9. Serve in your favorite bowl and sprinkle with chopped cilantro.

Serves: 12

Calories: 210 per serving

Chicken Dill 'N Dunk Marina

Transform this famous finger food into a gourmet dinner everyone

will crave for.

Ingredients

¼ kilo chicken breast tenders, cut into strips

1 large organic egg

6 tbsp. bread crumbs

1 ½ tbsp. olive oil, divide into two

¼ cup carrot, peeled and grated

¼ cup white mushrooms, finely chopped

1 clove minced garlic

1 small onion, chopped

½ cup zucchini, grated

¼ cup tomatoes, crushed

2 tbsp. flour (whole-wheat)

1 tbsp. fresh dill, chopped

½ tsp. oregano, dried

ground black pepper and salt to taste

Procedure

1. Preheat oven to 375°F.

2. While waiting for the oven to set, heat the olive oil on a non-stick skillet over medium fire. Add onions and sauté until golden.

3. Add the carrots and mushrooms cook for about 5 minutes.

4. Add garlic, zucchini, and pepper. Then tomatoes and oregano. Stir occasionally until veggies are softened.

5. Remove from the pan and transfer to a blender. Mix until you achieved your preferred consistency for the dip. Set aside.

6. Place the mixture of pepper, and salt on a large plate and then bread crumbs and dill on the other plate.

7. Take a large bowl and whisk together the egg and with 2-3 tbsp. of water.

8. Now it's time for the dry-wet-dry technique. Roll 1 chicken on the flour mixture, then to the egg mixture, and dredge over breadcrumbs and place on a baking sheet lined with parchment paper. Continue the process with the remaining chicken tenders.

9. Heat oil in large skillet over medium-high fire. Cook each side of the chicken until golden. Repeat with all chicken tenders.

10. Bake the fried chicken in the oven for another 5 minutes.

11. Serve with the homemade sauce

Serves: 9

Calories: 107 per serving

Irish Ragoût

Control your diabetes and have stronger bones with this Irish Ragoût or stew.

Ingredients

½ kilo lamb, boneless and cut into pieces

2 cups beef broth

½ kilo Burbank potatoes, cut into slices

¼ kilo carrots, sliced

¼ cup parsnips, sliced

¾ cups fresh peas

¼ cup onions, finely chopped

1tbsp. fresh parsley leaves, finely chopped

½ tsp. ground black pepper

½ tsp. salt to taste

Procedure

1. Set oven at 250°F.

2. Boil lamb with onions, potatoes, carrots, and parsnips in a large pot.

3. Sprinkle with salt and pepper. Let it simmer then transfer to the oven.

4. Bake for about 2 hours, until the rich scent fill the kitchen.

5. Let the stew cool down for a few minutes and serve with parsley on top.

Serves: 5

Calories: 273 per serving

Aloha Skewers

Enjoy these fruity and meaty skewers for your meals.

Ingredients

1/4 kilo fresh pineapple, cut into cubes

½ kilo chicken breast, cubed

6 cherry tomatoes, rinsed and sliced

½ tbsp rice wine vinegar

1 onion, chopped

1 1/2 tsp. honey, raw

1 regular ginger, grated and divided

½ tbsp soy sauce

For the sauce:

½ kilo fresh pineapple, cubed

1 lime, zested and freshly squeezed

1 lemon, zested and squeezed

½ tbsp. honey

½ tsp. grated ginger

Procedure

1. Preheat an indoor grill.

2. Whisk together last four ingredients in a large bowl. Add chicken breast then cover.

3. Marinate in the fridge for about an hour.

4. For the sauce, place all ingredients into a food processor, until smoothly blended. Set aside.

5. Remove the marinated chicken from the refrigerator and drain.

6. Alternate chicken breast with cubed pineapples, dividing evenly on 6 skewers.

7. Grill until the chicken is cooked through

8. Serve.

Serves: 6

Calories: 80 per serving

Butterflied grilled chicken with chile-lime rub

Ingredients

- 2 tablespoons of extra-virgin olive oil

- 3 tablespoons of lime juice

- 1 teaspoon of ground coriander

- 1 teaspoon of dried oregano, preferably Mexican

- 1 teaspoon of freshly ground pepper

- 1 chicken

- 3 tablespoons of chile powder

- 2 teaspoons of freshly grated lime zest

- 1 tablespoon of minced garlic

- 1 teaspoon of ground cumin

- 1 ½ teaspoons of kosher salt

- Pinch of ground cinnamon

Procedure

Combine paprika or chile powder, oil, cinnamon, pepper, salt, oregano, cumin, coriander, garlic, lime zest and juice in a small bowl to create a wet paste.

Cut the chicken with kitchen shears on one side of its backbone, across the ribs. Cut the opposite side similarly and remove the backbone. Discard or save it for your stock. Place down with the cut side facing down and flatten using the heel of your hand. Smear a generous amount of the spice rub around the skin and the interior of the chicken.

Slide into a microwave friendly baking dish. Cover using plastic wrap and place in the refrigerator to stay overnight or for twenty-four hours.

Preheat grill to medium-high heat halfway, and leave the other side unheated.

Let the spice rub stay on the chicken, and place it on the grill with the skin side facing down until it starts coloring and forms char marks, approximately five minutes. Turn over then grill for five more minutes. Transfer to the unheated side of the grill and close the lid. Cook for thirty to forty minutes. Place onto a platter, allow to cool for five minutes, and then serve.

Servings: 6

5 Chapter 5: Bonus Smoothies and Dessert Recipes

Choco cinnamon pudding

Ingredients

- 2 tablespoons of sugar

- 1 teaspoon of cinnamon

- 2 ½ cups of fat-free milk

- ¼ cup of cornstarch

- 3 tablespoons of unsweetened cocoa

- 1 ounce of dark chocolate, sliced into small pieces

Procedure

Put all the ingredients in a saucepan, except the milk and heat over medium heat. Gradually stir in the milk, stirring constantly. Bring the mixture to a boil, and then boil again for one minute. Continue stirring.

Remove from heat and place in the fridge to cool before eating.

Servings: 4

Coconut cranberry cookies

Yields: 40 cookies

Ingredients

- 1 teaspoon of baking soda

- ½ cup of fat-free vanilla yogurt

- 1 tablespoon of ground flaxseed

- 1 cup of dried cranberries

- 2 cups of whole-wheat flour

- ½ cup of vegetable oil

- 1 ½ cup of agave syrup

- 1 cup of sweetened shredded coconut

Procedure

Preheat oven to 350 degrees F. Spread a thin layer of coconut on a cookie sheet, and toast in the preheated oven for ten minutes. Raise the temperature to 375 degrees F.

Mix the baking soda and flours and whisk together. Mix the syrup, yogurt, and oil using an electric mixer until fluffy. Stir in the flaxseed, and then fold in the toasted cranberries and coconut.

Scoop a tablespoon of the mixture onto a clean cookie sheet, and bake for eight to ten minutes.

Servings: 40 cookies

JOHN BROWN

Hazelnut-Choco Balls

Don't be afraid for a choco dessert when on your clean eating diet. This no-cook recipe is less than 200 calories which you can store in fridge so you can just grab it when you crave for it.

Ingredients

2 cups hazelnut flour

1 cup hazelnuts, finely chopped

6 tbsp. dark chocolate, unsweetened

1 cup sour cherries, dried

1 ½ cups honey

1/2 cup coconut flour

2 tbsp. chia seeds (flaxseed if preferred)

1 tsp. vanilla extract

3 tsp. sesame seeds

1 cup rolled oats, old-fashioned

Procedure

1. In a blender, combine all ingredients except for oats. After a few seconds, add oats and blend for one more minute.

2. Put mixture in a large mixing bowl.

3. Wrap in plastic foil and freeze for about half an hour.

4. With your clean hands, shape the frozen mixture into small balls.

5. Place hazelnut-choco balls in an airtight container.

6. Munch and store the left overs the fridge.

Serves: 60

Calories: 151 per serving

Banana and Cherry Smoothie

Banana and Cherry a perfect flavor for a filling drink!

Ingredients

4 cups cherries, unsweetened

1 banana, chilled

4 cups green tea

½ cup prune juice

4 tbsp. yogurt

2 tbsp. chia seeds

Procedure

1. Mix all ingredients to a blender.

2. Add ice gradually as desired.

3. Blend until smooth.

4. Serve.

Serves: 2

Calories: 228 per serving

Rouge Flaxseed Smoothie

A no-sweat smoothie that you can prepare even on a day.

Ingredients

4 cups cherries, frozen and unsweetened

1 cup almonds. ground

1 cup freshly squeezed orange juice

4 tbsp. flaxseed

½ cup almonds, chopped

1 tsp. almond extract

Procedure

1. Put all ingredients except almonds in a food processor. Blend until smooth in texture.

2. Pour into choice of glass and sprinkle with almonds.

Serves: 4

Calories: 296 per serving

6 Chapter 6: Amazingly Clean Eating Recipes To Start Your Weight Loss Diet While Increasing Energy and Feeling Great!

Since, you have plentiful knowledge of clean eating you must be needing clean eating recipes to get started with. So here come completely clean breakfast, lunch and dinner recipes to give you a great start. Enjoy scrumptious and healthy food prepared by you!

Day 1

Breakfast

Mixed Berries Milkshake

Yield: 1 serving

Preparation Time: 10 minutes

Ingredients

½ cup frozen blackberries

½ cup frozen strawberries

½ cup frozen blueberries

3 Medjool dates, pitted and chopped

¾ cup unsweetened almond milk

Procedure

1. In a high speed blender, add all ingredients and pulse till smooth.

2. Serve immediately.

Lunch

Beans & Corn Salad

Yield: 2 servings

Preparation Time: 15 minutes

Ingredients

¼ cup canned black beans, rinsed and drained

¼ cup canned red kidney beans, rinsed and drained

¼ cup corn kernels

¼ cup cherry tomatoes, halved

¼ cup avocado, peeled, pitted and cubed

2 cups romaine lettuce, torn

1 tablespoon fresh lemon juice

Salt and freshly ground black pepper, to taste

Procedure

1. In a serving bowl, add all ingredients and gently toss to coat well.

2. Serve immediately.

Dinner

Steak & Veggie Salad

Yield: 4 servings

Preparation Time: 20 minutes

Cooking Time: 6-10 minutes

Ingredients

1¾ pounds beef sirloin steak

Salt and freshly ground black pepper, to taste

1 large green bell pepper, seeded and sliced thinly

1 large carrot, peeled and sliced thinly

2 tomatoes, chopped

½ cup red onion, sliced

8 cups romaine lettuce

¼ cup extra-virgin olive oil

2 tablespoons fresh lemon juice

2 tablespoons red wine vinegar

1 teaspoon Worcestershire sauce

1 garlic clove, minced

2 tablespoons fresh cilantro, minced

Procedure

1. Preheat grill for high heat. Grease the grill grate.

2. Sprinkle the steak with a little salt and black pepper.

3. Grill for about 3-5 minutes from both sides or until desired doneness.

4. Transfer the steak onto a cutting board and let it cool.

5. With a sharp knife, cut the steak into desired slices.

6. In a large bowl, mix together bell pepper, carrot, tomato, onion and lettuce.

7. In a small bowl, add oil, lemon juice, vinegar, Worcestershire sauce, garlic, cilantro, salt and black pepper and beat till well combined.

8. Place steak over salad and drizzle with dressing.

9. Serve immediately.

Day 2

Breakfast

Creamy Healthy Smoothie

Yield: 1 serving

Preparation Time: 10 minutes

Ingredients

¼ of avocado, peeled, pitted and chopped

½ of banana, peeled and sliced

½ cup fresh blueberries

1 cup fresh spinach

¼ of cucumber, peeled and chopped

1½ teaspoons hemp seeds, shelled

¼ teaspoon wheatgrass powder

1 cup coconut water

Procedure

In a high speed blender, add all ingredients and pulse till smooth.

Serve immediately.

Lunch

Pasta & Veggie Salad

Yield: 10 servings

Preparation Time: 20 minutes

Cooking Time: 8-10 minutes

Ingredients

2 cups whole-wheat tri color rotini pasta

¼ cup balsamic vinegar

¼ cup extra-virgin olive oil

1 teaspoon raw honey

2 garlic cloves, minced

Salt and freshly ground black pepper, to taste

2 large carrots, peeled and chopped

1 large cucumber, peeled and chopped

1 cup celery, chopped

2 Roma tomatoes, chopped

1 red onion, chopped

2 scallions, chopped

2 tablespoons fresh cilantro, chopped

2 tablespoons fresh parsley, chopped

Procedure

1. In a large pan of lightly salted boiling water, add pasta and cook for about 8-10 minutes or according to package's directions.

2. Drain and rinse under cold water. Drain well and transfer into a large bowl.

3. In another bowl, add vinegar, oil, honey, garlic, salt and black pepper and beat till well combined.

4. Add dressing in the bowl with pasta. Add remaining ingredients and stir to combine.

5. Serve immediately.

Dinner

Chicken & Vegetables Soup

Yield: 4 servings

Preparation Time: 15 minutes

Cooking Time: 20 minutes

Ingredients

1 tablespoon extra-virgin olive oil

1 small carrot, peeled and chopped

½ cup onion, chopped

1 celery stalk, chopped

2 garlic cloves, minced

½ teaspoon ground cumin

¼ teaspoon red pepper flakes, crushed

1¼ cups zucchini, sliced

5 cups fat-free, low- sodium chicken broth

1¼ cups cooked chicken, chopped

2 cups fresh kale, trimmed and chopped

Salt and freshly ground black pepper, to taste

2 tablespoons fresh lime juice

2 tablespoons fresh cilantro, chopped

Procedure

1.	In a large soup pan, heat oil on medium heat.

2.	Add carrot, onion and celery and sauté for about 8-9 minutes.

3.	Add garlic and spices and sauté for about 1 minute.

4.	Add zucchini and broth and bring to a boil on high heat. Reduce the heat to medium-low.

5.	Simmer for about 5 minutes.

6.	Add cooked chicken and kale and simmer for about 5 minutes.

7.	Stir in salt, black pepper and lime juice and remove from heat.

8.	Serve hot with the garnishing of cilantro

Day 3

Breakfast

Feta Spinach Omelet

Yield:2 servings

Preparation Time: 15 minutes

Cooking Time:6½ minutes

Ingredients

4 large eggs

¼ cup cooked spinach, squeezed

2 scallions, chopped

2 tablespoons fresh parsley, chopped

½ cup feta cheese, crumbled

Freshly ground black pepper, to taste

2 teaspoons extra-virgin olive oil

Procedure

1. Preheat the broiler of oven. Arrange a rack about 4-inches from heating element.

2. In a bowl, crack the eggs and beat well.

3. Add remaining ingredients except oil and stir to combine.

4. In an ovenproof skillet, heat oil on medium heat.

5. Add egg mixture and tilt the skillet to spread the mixture evenly.

6. Immediately, reduce the heat to medium-low.

7. Cook for about 3-4 minutes or till golden brown.

8. Now, transfer the skillet under broiler and broil for about 1½-2½ minutes.

9. Cut the omelet into desired size wedges and serve.

Lunch

Green Veggies Soup

Yield: 4 servings

Preparation Time: 20 minutes

Cooking Time: 3-4 minutes

Ingredients

¼ cup almonds, soaked for overnight and drained

1 large avocado, peeled, pitted and chopped

½ small green bell pepper, seeded and chopped

2 cups fresh spinach leaves

1 small zucchini, chopped

2 celery stalks, chopped

2 tablespoons onion, chopped

1 garlic clove, chopped

½ cup fresh cilantro leaves

¼ cup fresh parsley leaves

2 tablespoons fresh lemon juice

Salt and freshly ground black pepper, to taste

2 cups vegetable fat-free, low- sodium broth

Procedure

1. In a high speed blender, add all ingredients and pulse till smooth.

2. Transfer the soup into a pan and cook on medium heat for 3-4 minutes or heated through.

3. Serve immediately.

Dinner

Noodles & Mixed Vegetables Soup

Yield: 4 servings

Preparation Time: 20 minutes

Cooking Time: 15 minutes

Ingredients

8-ounce whole wheat pasta (of your choice)

1 tablespoon extra-virgin olive oil

1 tablespoon fresh ginger, grated finely

1 jalapeño pepper, chopped

6-ounces fresh shiitake mushrooms, sliced thinly

¼ cup low-sodium soy sauce

4½ cups vegetable fat-free, low- sodium broth

3 carrots, peeled and julienned

6-ounce fresh green beans, trimmed and cut into 2-inch pieces

3 scallions, sliced

Procedure

1. In a large pan of lightly salted boiling water, cook the noodles for about 8-10 minutes or according to package's directions.

2. Drain well and keep aside.

3. Meanwhile in a large soup pan, heat oil on medium heat.

4. Add ginger and jalapeño pepper and sauté for about 1 minute.

5. Add mushrooms and cook for about 4-5 minutes.

6. Add soy sauce and broth and bring to a boil.

7. Stir in remaining vegetables and again bring to a boil.

8. Reduce the heat to medium-low.

9. Simmer for about 6-8 minutes or till desired doneness.

10. Divide the noodles in 4 serving bowls

11. Pour hot soup over noodles and serve immediately.

Day 4

Breakfast

Eggs with Vegetables

Yield: 4 servings

Preparation Time: 15 minutes

Cooking Time: 17 minutes

Ingredients

1 cup fresh green beans, trimmed and cut into 1-inch pieces

2 tablespoons extra-virgin olive oil

2 pounds boiling potatoes, sliced

2 garlic cloves, minced

1 jalapeño pepper, seeded and chopped

Pinch of red pepper flakes, crushed

Salt and freshly ground black pepper, to taste

4 eggs

Procedure

1. In a large pan of boiling water, add green beans and cook for about 3 minutes or till crisp.

2. Drain well and rinse under cold running water.

3. In a large nonstick skillet, heat oil on medium heat.

4. Place potato slices in the bottom of skillet in an even layer.

5. Cook for about 10-12 minutes, flipping occasionally.

6. Stir in remaining ingredients and except eggs.

7. Carefully, crack the eggs over veggie mixture.

8. Cover the skillet and cook for about 3-5 minutes.

9. Serve immediately.

Lunch

Tofu & Oats Burgers

Yield: 4 servings

Preparation Time: 15 minutes

Cooking Time: 16-20 minutes

Ingredients

1 pound firm tofu, pressed and crumbled

¾ cup rolled oats

¼ cup flaxseeds

2 cups frozen spinach, thawed and squeezed

1 medium onion, chopped finely

2 garlic cloves, minced

1 jalapeño pepper, seeded and minced

1 teaspoon ground cumin

½ teaspoon red pepper flakes, crushed

Salt and freshly ground black pepper, to taste

2 tablespoons extra-virgin olive oil

6 cups mixed fresh baby greens

Procedure

1. In a large bowl, mix together all ingredients except oil and salad greens. Keep aside for 10 minutes.

2. Make desired size patties from mixture.

3. In a nonstick frying pan, heat oil on medium heat.

4. Cook patties for 8-10 minutes per side.

5. Serve these patties with fresh greens.

Dinner

Tofu with Three Peas

Servings: 6

Preparation Time: 15 minutes

CookingTime: 18 minutes

Ingredients

1 tablespoon chile garlic sauce

3 tablespoons low-sodium soy sauce

2 tablespoonsextra-virgin olive oil, divided

1 (16-ounce) package extra-firm tofu, drained, pressed and cubed

1 cup onion, chopped

1 tablespoon fresh ginger, minced

2 garlic cloves, minced

1 cup frozen peas, thawed

2½ cups snow peas, trimmed

2½ cups sugar snap peas, trimmed

Procedure

1. In a bowl, mix together chile garlic sauce and soy sauce.

2. In a large skillet, heat 1 tablespoon of oil on medium-high heat.

3. Add tofu and cook, stirring occasionally for about 6-8 minutes or till browned completely.

4. Transfer the tofu into a bowl

5. In the same skillet, heat remaining oil on medium heat.

6. Add onion and sauté for about 3-4 minutes.

7. Add ginger and garlic and sauté for about 1 minute.

8. Stir in all three peas and cook for about 2-3 minutes.

9. Stir in sauce mixture and tofu and cook for about 1-2 minutes.

10. Serve hot.

Day 5

Breakfast

Bell Pepper Frittata

Yield:6 servings

Preparation Time: 15 minutes

Cooking Time:7 minutes

Ingredients

8 eggs

1 tablespoon fresh cilantro, chopped

1 tablespoon fresh basil, chopped

¼ teaspoon red pepper flakes, crushed

Salt and freshly ground black pepper, to taste

2 tablespoons extra-virgin olive oil

1 bunch scallions, chopped

1 cup red bell pepper, seeded and sliced thinly

½ cup goat cheese, crumbled

Procedure

1. Preheat the broiler of oven. Arrange a rack in upper third of oven.

2. In a bowl, add eggs, fresh herbs, red pepper flakes, salt and black pepper and beat well.

3. In an ovenproof skillet, heat oil on medium heat.

4. Add scallion and bell pepper and sauté for about 1 minute.

5. Add egg mixture over bell pepper mixture evenly and lift the edges to let the egg mixture flow underneath and cook for about 2-3 minutes.

6. Place the cheese on top in the form of dots.

7. Now, transfer the skillet under broiler and broil for about 2-3 minutes.

8. Cut the frittata into desired size slices and serve.

Lunch

Chicken Kebabs with Salad

Yield: 4 servings

Preparation Time: 15 minutes

Cooking Time: 6 minutes

Ingredients

For Kebabs:

1 teaspoon garlic, minced

1 tablespoon fresh thyme, minced

2 tablespoons fresh lemon juice

1 tablespoon extra-virgin olive oil

Salt and freshly ground black pepper, to taste

4 (6-ounce) skinless, boneless chicken breasts, cubed into ½-inch size

For Salad:

2 cups grape tomatoes, halved

1 red onion, chopped

6 cups lettuce leaves, torn

1 garlic clove, minced

2 tablespoons fresh cilantro, minced

2 tablespoons fresh lemon juice

2 tablespoons extra-virgin olive oil

Salt and freshly ground black pepper, to taste

Procedure

1. For chicken in a large bowl, mix together all ingredients except chicken cubes.

2. Add chicken cubes ant coat with marinade generously.

3. Cover and refrigerate to marinate for at least 2 hours.

4. Preheat grill to high heat. Grease the grill grate.

5. Remove the chicken from refrigerator and thread onto pre-soaked wooden skewers.

6. Grill for about 6-8 minutes, flipping occasionally or till desired doneness.

7. Meanwhile in a large bowl, mix together tomatoes, onion and

    lettuce.

8. In another bowl, add remaining ingredients and beat till well

    combined.

9. Pour dressing over salad and toss to coat.

10. Serve chicken kebabs with salad.

Dinner

Grilled Chicken Thighs

Yield: 4 servings

Preparation Time: 15 minutes

Cooking Time: 16 minutes

Ingredients

1 tablespoons fresh lime juice

½ tablespoon fresh thyme, minced

½ tablespoon fresh oregano, minced

½ teaspoon ground cumin

½ tablespoon red pepper flakes, crushed

¼ tablespoon paprika

1/8 teaspoon onion powder

1/8 teaspoon garlic powder

Salt and freshly ground black pepper, to taste

4 (4-ounce) skinless, boneless chicken thighs

For Serving:

8 cups fresh baby spinach

Procedure

1. Preheat the grill to medium-high heat. Grease the grill grate.

2. For chicken in a bowl, add all ingredients except chicken thighs and mix till well combined.

3. Coat the thighs with spice mixture generously.

4. Grill for about 8 minutes from both sides.

5. Serve the grilled thighs with spinach.

Day 6

Breakfast

Lemony Strawberry French Toasts

Yield:2 servings

Preparation Time: 10 minutes

Cooking Time:5 minutes

Ingredients

2 egg whites

½ teaspoon ground cinnamon

1½ teaspoons pure vanilla extract

2 grain-free bread slices

2 teaspoons butter

1 cup frozen strawberries

¼ teaspoon powdered stevia

3 teaspoons fresh lemon juice

Procedure

1. In a bowl, add egg whites, cinnamon and vanilla and beat well.

2. Add bread slices in the egg white mixture and coat from both sides evenly.

3. In a nonstick skillet, melt butter on medium heat.

4. Add slices and cook for about 5 minutes, flipping once in the middle way or till golden brown from both sides.

5. Meanwhile in a small nonstick pan, add strawberries on low heat.

6. Cook for about 2-3 minutes.

7. Stir in stevia lemon juice and remove from heat.

8. Top the French toasts with strawberry mixture and serve.

Lunch

Shrimp Rolls

Yield: 6 servings

Preparation Time: 20 minutes

Ingredients:

1-ounce cellophane noodles

1 tablespoon white vinegar

6 spring roll wrappers

12 medium cooked shrimp, peeled, deveined and halved lengthwise

2 medium carrots, peeled and julienned

½ cup green cabbage, shredded

½ cup red cabbage, shredded

1 medium seedless cucumber, julienned

1 avocado, peeled, pitted and sliced

1 head Boston lettuce, torn

2 tablespoons fresh cilantro, chopped

2 tablespoons fresh basil, chopped

Procedure

1. In a pan of boiling water, place cellophane and keep aside for 10 minutes.

2. Drain well and transfer into a bowl.

3. Add vinegar and toss to coat and keep aside.

4. In a large round pie plate, pour hot water. Place the each wrapper for about for 15-30 seconds or till soft.

5. Meanwhile in a large bowl, mix together remaining all ingredients.

6. Place each wrapper onto a large piece of parchment paper.

7. Divide shrimp mixture over the center of wrapper evenly, leaving at least an inch on the sides.

8. Carefully, fold the bottom edge of wrapper over the filling and roll tightly.

9. Secure each wrap with toothpick and serve.

Dinner

Veggie Stuffed Chicken Breasts

Yield: 8 servings

Preparation Time: 15 minutes

Cooking Time: 12 minutes

Ingredients:

1 large red bell pepper, seeded and chopped finely

2 tablespoons kalamata olives, pitted and chopped finely

1 tablespoon fresh parsley, minced

¼ cup feta cheese, crumbled

8 (6-ounce) skinless, boneless chicken breast halves

Salt and freshly ground black pepper, to taste

Procedure

1. Preheat grill for medium-high heat. Grease the grill grate.

2. In a bowl, mix together all ingredients except chicken breasts and seasoning.

3. With a sharp knife, make a horizontal slit in each breast half to form a pocket.

4. Fill each pocket with vegetable mixture evenly and secure with toothpicks.

5. Sprinkle with salt and black pepper evenly,

6. Grill for about 6 minutes from both sides or till desired doneness.

Day 7

Breakfast

Fruity Oat Muffins

Yield: 5 servings

Preparation Time: 15 minutes

Cooking Time: 12 minutes

Ingredients:

½ cup rolled oats

¼ cup almond flour

½ teaspoon baking soda

2 tablespoons flaxseeds

½ teaspoon ground cinnamon

Pinch of ground nutmeg

1 egg

¼ cup unsalted butter, softened

2 tablespoons banana, peeled and sliced

½ teaspoon vanilla extract

¼ cup fresh blueberries

Procedure

1. Preheat the oven to 375 degrees F. Grease 10 cups of a muffin tray.

2. In a blender, add all ingredients except blueberries and pulse till smooth and creamy.

3. Transfer the mixture into a bowl and gently, fold in blueberries.

4. Transfer the mixture into prepared muffin cups evenly.

5. Bake for about 10-12 minutes or till a toothpick inserted in the center comes out clean.

Lunch

Lemony Quinoa & Green Beans

Yield:4 servings

Preparation Time: 10 minutes

Cooking Time: 20 minutes

Ingredients:

2 tablespoons extra-virgin olive oil, divided

1 small onion, chopped

2 garlic cloves, minced

1 Serrano pepper, seeded and chopped finely

1 cup quinoa

Salt and freshly ground black pepper, to taste

1¾ cups fat-free, low- sodium vegetable broth

1 pound fresh green beans, trimmed and cut into 2-inch pieces

2 tablespoons fresh lemon juice

Procedure

1. In a pan, heat 1 tablespoon of oil on medium heat.

2. Add onion and sauté for about 2-3 minutes.

3. Add garlic and Serrano pepper and sauté for about 1 minute.

4. Add quinoa and cook, stirring continuously for about 1 minute.

5. Add salt, black pepper and broth and bring to a boil.

6. Reduce the heat to low. Cover and simmer for about 15 minutes.

7. Remove from heat and keep aside, covered for about 10 minutes. With a fork, fluff the quinoa.

8. Meanwhile in a pan of salted boiling water, add beans and cook for about 4-5 minutes or till crisp tender.

9. In a large serving bowl, mix together quinoa and green beans. Sprinkle with a little salt and black pepper.

10. Drizzle with lemon juice and remaining oil and serve.

Dinner

Simple Grilled Beef Steak

Yield: 8 servings

Preparation Time: 15 minutes

Cooking Time: 8-10 minutes

Ingredients

4 (½-pound) grass-fed beef top sirloin steaks

2 tablespoons extra-virgin olive oil

2 tablespoons steak seasoning

Procedure

1. Preheat the grill for high heat. Grease the grill grate.

2. In a large bowl, mix together oil and seasoning mix and coat the steaks with mixture generously.

3. Grill the steak for about 4-5 minutes per side or till desired doneness.

4. Cut each steak in half and serve.

Day 8

Breakfast

Baked Cherry Pancakes

Yield:4 servings

Preparation Time: 15 minutes

Cooking Time:15-20 minutes

Ingredients

1 teaspoon unsalted butter

½ cup whole-wheat pastry flour

1/8 teaspoon ground cinnamon

Pinch of salt

3 eggs

½ cup fat-free milk

1 tablespoon unsalted butter, melted

1 teaspoon vanilla extract

2 cups fresh sweet cherries, pitted and halved

¼ cup almonds, chopped

Procedure

1. Preheat the oven to 450 degrees F.

2. In a 10-inch ovenproof skillet, add 1 teaspoon of butter and place the skillet into oven.

3. In a bowl, mix together flour, cinnamon and salt.

4. In another bowl, add eggs, milk, butter and vanilla and beat till well combined.

5. Add egg mixture into flour mixture and mix till well combined.

6. Remove the skillet from oven and tilt to spread the melted butter evenly.

7. Place cherries in the bottom of skillet in a single layer.

8. Place the flour mixture over cherries evenly

9. Top with almonds evenly.

10. Bake for about 15-20 minutes or till a toothpick inserted in the center comes out clean.

11. Remove from oven and let it cool for at least 5 minutes before slicing.

12. Cut into 4 equal sized wedges and serve.

Lunch

Spinach & Tofu Stir Fry

Yield:2 servings

Preparation Time: 10 minutes

Cooking Time: 15 minutes

Ingredients

2 tablespoons extra-virgin olive oil

1 medium onion, chopped

2 garlic cloves, minced

2 teaspoons fresh basil, chopped

½ pound firm tofu, pressed and cubed

4 cups fresh spinach, chopped

Salt and freshly ground black pepper, to taste

1 tablespoon fresh lemon juice

Procedure

1. In a large skillet, heat oil on medium heat.

2. Add onion and sauté for about 3-4 minutes.

3. Add garlic and basil and sauté for about 1 minute.

4. Add tofu and stir fry for about 5-6 minutes.

5. Add spinach, salt and black pepper and stir fry for about 3-4 minutes.

6. Stir in lemon juice and remove from heat.

7. Serve hot.

Dinner

Pork with Bok Choy

Yield: 4 servings

Preparation Time: 15 minutes

Cooking Time: 18 minutes

Ingredients

1 tablespoon extra-virgin olive oil

4 scallions, chopped

2 garlic cloves, minced

2 tablespoons fresh ginger, minced

1 Serrano pepper, chopped finely

1 pound pork loin steaks, trimmed and cut into strips

3 tablespoons low-sodium soy sauce

½ pound bokchoy, sliced

Procedure

1. In a large skillet, heat oil on medium heat.

2. Add scallion and sauté for about 2 minutes.

3. Add garlic, ginger and Serrano pepperand sauté for about 1 minute.

4. Add pork and cook for about 8-10 minutes or till tender.

5. Add soy sauce and bok choy and cook for about 4-5 minutes.

6. Serve hot.

Day 9

Breakfast

Quinoa & Date Bowl

Yield: 4 servings

Preparation Time: 10 minutes

Cooking Time: 10-15 minutes

Ingredients

2 cups unsweetened almond milk

1 cup quinoa

¼ teaspoon vanilla extract

Pinch of ground cinnamon

2 Medjool dates, pitted and chopped very finely

1 cup fresh strawberries, hulled and sliced

Procedure

1. In a pan, mix together milk, quinoa, vanilla and cinnamon on low heat.

2. Cook, stirring occasionally for about 10-15 minutes.

3. Stir in chopped dates and immediately, remove from heat.

4. Serve with the garnishing of strawberries.

Lunch

Broth Braised Cabbage

Yield: 4 servings

Preparation Time: 15 minutes

Cooking Time: 25 minutes

Ingredients

1½ teaspoons extra-virgin olive oil

2 garlic cloves, minced

3 cups green cabbage, chopped

1 onion, sliced thinly

1 cup fat-free, low- sodium vegetable broth

Salt and freshly ground black pepper, to taste

Procedure

1. In a large nonstick skillet, heat oil on high heat.

2. Add garlic and sauté for about1 minute.

3. Add cabbage and onion and sauté for about 3-4 minutes.

4. Stir in broth, salt and black pepper and immediately, reduce the heat to low.

5. Cover and cook for about 20 minutes.

6. Serve warm.

Dinner

Grilled Lamb Chops & Veggies

Yield: 8 servings

Preparation Time: 15 minutes

Cooking Time: 15 minutes

Ingredients

For Chops:

¼ cup balsamic vinegar

3 tablespoons extra-virgin olive oil

2 tablespoons fresh lemon juice

4 minced garlic cloves

2 teaspoons dried rosemary, crushed

Salt and freshly ground black pepper, as required

8 (1-inch thick) lamb chops

ForVeggies:

32 fresh cherry tomatoes, stemmed

1½ pounds asparagus, trimmed

2 tablespoons olive oil

2 teaspoons minced fresh parsley

2 teaspoons minced freshrosemary

Salt and freshly ground black pepper, as required

Procedure

1. In a large bowl, mix together oil, vinegar, lemon juice, garlic, rosemary, salt and black pepper.

2. Add chops and coat with marinade generously. Cover and refrigerate to marinate for about 4-5 hours.

3. Remove from refrigerator and keep in room temperature for at least 30 minutes.

4. Preheat the grill to medium-high heat. Grease the grill grate.

5. Cook the chops for about 4 minutes per side.

6. Transfer the chops into a large plate. Cover with foil paper to keep them warm.

7. Meanwhile for vegetables in a large bowl, add all ingredients and toss to coat well.

8. Thread the cherry tomatoes onto presoaked wooden skewers.

9. After removing chops from grill, grease the grill grate again.

10. Grill the tomatoes for about 3-4 minutes per side.

11. Now, increase the temperature of grill to high heat.

12. Grill the asparagus for about 2-3 minutes.

13. Divide the chops, tomatoes and asparagus in 8 serving plates evenly and serve.

Day 10

Breakfast

Nutty Oatmeal

Yield: 4 servings

Preparation Time: 10 minutes

Cooking Time: 3-4 minutes

Ingredients

1 cup steel cut oats

2 cups unsweetened almond milk, divided

4-6 drops liquid stevia

1 large banana, peeled and sliced

¼ cup walnuts, chopped

Procedure

1. In a bowl, add oats, 1 cup of milk and stevia and stir well.

2. Cover and refrigerate for at least overnight.

3. Remove from refrigerator. Transfer the oats mixture into a pan on medium heat.

4. Add remaining milk and stir to combine.

5. Cook for 3-4 minutes or till heated completely.

6. Transfer oat mixture into serving bowls.

7. Top with banana slices and walnuts and serve.

Lunch

Shrimp in Sweet & Sour Sauce

Yield: 2 servings

Preparation Time: 15 minutes

Cooking Time: 10 minutes

Ingredients

For Sauce:

3 tablespoons fresh orange juice

1 tablespoon organic honey

1 tablespoon low-sodium soy sauce

½ tablespoon balsamic vinegar

For Shrimp:

¾ pound shrimp, peeled and deveined

½ tablespoons arrowroot powder

1 tablespoon extra-virgin olive oil

2 garlic cloves, minced

1 teaspoon fresh ginger, minced

Procedure

1. In a bowl, mix together all sauce ingredients. Keep aside.

2. In a bowl, add shrimp and sprinkle with arrowroot powder and toss to coat well.

3. In a large skillet, heat oil on medium-high heat.

4. Add garlic and ginger and sauté for about 1 minute.

5. Add shrimp and cook for about 3 minutes.

6. Add sauce and cook, stirring continuously for about 2 minutes.

7. With a slotted spoon, transfer the shrimp into a bowl.

8. Cook, stirring for about 2-4 minutes or till desired thickness.

9. Serve shrimp with the topping of sauce.

Dinner

Salmon & Veggie Parcel

Yield: 6 servings

Preparation Time: 15 minutes

Cooking Time: 20 minutes

Ingredients

6 (3-ounce) salmon fillets

Salt and freshly ground black pepper, to taste

1 yellow bell pepper, seeded and sliced thinly

1 red bell pepper, seeded and sliced thinly

4 plum tomatoes, sliced thinly

1 small onion, sliced thinly

½ cup fresh parsley, chopped

1/3 cup capers

¼ cup extra-virgin olive oil

2 tablespoons fresh lemon juice

Procedure

1. Preheat the oven to 400 degrees F.

2. Arrange 6 foil pieces of foil paper on smooth surface.

3. Place 1 salmon fillet on each foil paper. Sprinkle with salt and black pepper.

4. In a bowl, mix together bell peppers, tomato and onion.

5. Place veggie mixture over each fillet evenly.

6. Top with parsley and capers evenly.

7. Drizzle with oil and lemon juice.

8. Fold the foil paper around salmon mixture to seal it.

9. Arrange the foil packets onto a large baking sheet in a single layer.

10. Bake for about 20 minutes.

Conclusion

Thank you again for purchasing this book!

I hope this book was able to help you to know what you need to do for the next 30 days in order to boost your energy and remain healthy.

I included a extra Bonus book complete with 37 delicious quick and simple clean eating recipes. As my token of appreciate for downloading my book.

The next step is to start by getting rid of the foods that are lowering your energy levels and incorporate healthier foods as indicated in this book. All the best as you begin this journey.

Finally, if you enjoyed this book, would you be kind enough to leave a review for this book on Amazon?

Thank you and good luck! – John Brown

Made in the USA
San Bernardino, CA
16 December 2016